So, what's the

A journal for the curious.

Written and illustrated by
KMRaposa

Dartmouth, Massachusetts

KMRaposa.com
2019 all rights reserved

Copyright ©KMRaposa.com all rights reserved 2019

This book serves simply as a journal or workbook. It is written as a reference to what the author has experienced in her own life. References to real people, events, establishments, organizations, or locales are intended only to provide a sense of authenticity and are used fictitiously. All other characters, and all incidents and dialogue are drawn from the author's imagination and are not to be constructed as real. No information or advice written in this book is to be taken as fact or medical advice. This book provides information on energetic and spiritual beliefs. Do not take this book as an authentic diagnosis of any disease or disorder. The author does not discourage western medicine and encourages you to seek professional medical advice in all instances regarding health and well-being.

Originally published in 2018 in Dartmouth, Massachusetts.

So, what's the deal with chakras, anyway!? Copyright 2019 by KMRaposa.com. All rights reserved. Printed in the United States of America. No part o this book may be used or reproduced in any manner whatsoever without written permission from the author except brief quotations. For information regarding rights and permissions, contact www.kmraposa.com

Designed and illustrated by KMRaposa

Special Acknowledgements:

A special thank you to those who helped me along the way.
You are the empowered who empower others!

Sarah Moniz and Erin Poyant,
Owners of Solshine Yoga Studio in New Bedford, Ma
SolshineYoga.org

Nicole Lahousse
Empowerment Coach and owner of MajikLLC.com

Liz Lepage
Owner of Plum Direct Marketing
PlumDirectMarketing.com

Laurie Soares
Owner of Sensations Salon
Sensations1809.com

Jennifer Machado,
Owner of Studio 1194
Studio1194.com

Michelle Braga

Amy Gordon

Brittany DeMita

Caitlin Reed

Editing and concept credits to:
Daniela Andrade, Raelyn Monteiro, and Amanda Sexton
Writers and content creators at FoxxAndLuna.com

Copyright ©KMRaposa.com all rights reserved 2019

Additional thank you to the following businesses for being open to my ideas and supporting the publishing and resale of this book:

Solshine Yoga Studio New Bedford, MA
Sacred Lotus Westport, MA
Euphoria Day Spa Fairhaven, MA
Divine Massage Mattapoisett and New Bedford, MA
Strawberry Moon Dartmouth, MA
Divinely Balanced Holistic Healing New Bedford MA

Copyright ©KMRaposa.com all rights reserved 2019

For my favorite person.

Finally, I could not have achieved this goal, written or published this book without the constant encouragement and support from my other half. He is my partner in life and in business- my favorite person. Mike believed in my dreams before I could even clearly see them. He helped me identify my goals, organize a solid and clear plan, and saw me through every road block. This book would not be possible without his support, patience and love.

Copyright ©KMRaposa.com all rights reserved 2019

About the Author

Kelly Raposa was born in New Bedford, Massachusetts and now resides in Dartmouth. After several years in consumer banking, she was in search of something more fulfilling. She left banking to pursue a career in holistic wellness, managing a local holistic wellness center and crystal shop. Here, she learned about hundreds of crystals and their healing potential, as well as chakras, energies, reiki, yoga, meditation and more. After healing some old traumas and breaking negative thought patterns that held her back, Kelly became empowered to set out on her own as a business owner, writer and creator.

She currently owns Foxx and Luna Creative which supports local small businesses in their creative marketing and branding efforts.

KMRaposa.com

Copyright ©KMRaposa.com all rights reserved 2019

Introduction
Week 1: Root Chakra
Root Chakra Affirmations
Root Chakra Journaling
Root Chakra Mandala

Week 2: Sacral Chakra
Sacral Chakra Affirmations
Sacral Chakra Journaling
Sacral Chakra Mandala

Week 3: Solar Plexus Chakra
Solar Plexus Affirmations
Solar Plexus Journaling
Solar Plexus Mandala

Week 4: Heart Chakra
Heart Chakra Affirmations
Heart Chakra Journaling
Heart Chakra Mandala

Week 5: Throat Chakra
Throat Chakra Affirmations
Throat Chakra Journaling
Throat Chakra Mandala

Week 6: Third Eye Chakra
Third Eye Affirmations
Third Eye Journaling
Third Eye Mandala

Week 7: Crown Chakra
Crown Chakra Affirmations
Crown Chakra Journaling
Crown Chakra Mandala

So, what's the deal with Chakras, anyway!?

Copyright ©KMRaposa.com all rights reserved 2019

Introduction

Are you ready to begin your journey?

Copyright ©KMRaposa.com all rights reserved 2019

So, here's the skinny on "chakras." Prior to our modern life of science and technology, ancient cultures lived by the concept that every living being had a life force within them- centers of energy. Basically, these energy centers move inside of us and correlate with emotions, physical traits, mental health and more. These energy centers became known as "chakras" which is a Sanskrit word translating to "wheel." Energy centers also believed to exist outside of our physical bodies, but for the sake of this book, we will focus on 7 energy centers located inside of our bodies.

Here's the part where I include a disclaimer for the science people, the haters, the people who take things too literally, and the people who might think this book serves to replace your doctor or prescribed medications. This book is intended to provide information on ancient beliefs in energy and to share with you the path I have taken. This should, in no way, be taken as medical advice, as definite fact, or to replace your licensed doctors. I have found, personally, that meditating on the chakras and balancing my own energies has helped me. Meditation, energy work, herbal medicine, journaling, yoga, massage therapy, color therapy, art therapy and even crystal energy have all worked together to help me get where I am today. This book is just my way of passing on what worked for me.

For many years, I was medicated for depression, chronic anxiety, bipolar disorder and more. Medication did work for me- to some extent. But then I found my body rejecting the massive amounts of medications I was taking. I was sleeping more often than not, but when I wasn't sleeping, I was still in constant dream state. I know this sounds glamorous, but the fact of the matter is, I couldn't concentrate on life- on work- on my relationships. I lacked authentic emotion because I was so out of it. My senses, natural reactions and emotions were all being numbed. That numb feeling served me well when my father had passed away, or so I thought. Turns out, I never grieved my father's passing until years later when I weened myself off medication. I AM NOT DISQUALIFYING THE USE OF MEDICATION. I truly believe I needed some of those medications and without them, I may not be here today. I'm just saying there are alternatives. They might work for you. They are working for me. PLEASE DO NOT ABRUPTLY STOP TAKING YOUR PRESCRIBED MEDICATIONS. If you want to try this route, consult your physician first. Most of the time, they will slowly ween you off your medications. Be kind to yourself, to your body, and honor the process. Whole life transformation doesn't happen overnight.

Speaking of whole life transformation- mine started with a change in occupation- from good ole' consumer banking to working at a holistic energy center to eventually nannying and starting my own business. I had to let go of people who held me back. People who weren't on the same path and some whose negative energy affected me to the point where I could not grow with them around. I had to let go of a partner I was with for 7 years. I had to change my entire friend group. I had to even let go of family members that I love and will always love, but who just didn't fit the mold of my new life. Substance abuse is a pretty big issue in my family and in my old friend group, and I found it too difficult to constantly say no and refrain when it was around me, so the only solution was removing myself from those situations completely. See, even though I am not an alcoholic or addict, I think like one and I am still, to this day, working through these addictive behaviors and thought patterns. I tend to look for ways to escape or to numb negative feelings when things happen outside of my control. I have learned and am still learning to rely on natural, healthy methods to cope with negative situations. I'm a work in progress. THIS IS NOT EASY. This does not happen overnight. Honor the process. So, basically, during this time I discovered that through journaling we can identity why we do the things we do. Once we find the root of our actions, we can begin to change or improve our reactions. I've included journal prompts for each chakra to help you begin to understand each of your energy centers. Try to be as honest as possible when journaling. This is only for you- no one will see it but you!

After letting go of people and circumstances that no longer served me, I had to fix some other things. My diet, for one, was complete trash. Full of processed foods, sugars, and way too much coffee. But, hey, I'm human and if I'm honest with you, I'm still working on this. In fact, right now, I'm drinking coffee milk and eating Swedish fish. I never said I was a saint. I need you to understand that I am not better than you. I am not perfect. I have no idea what I'm doing most days. Every day is choice- a choice to live better, think positively, take care of yourself. And sometimes we fail. And sometimes we succeed. But we're human. If I can do anything, its to share tools with you that you can carry in your tool belt to help you get through those rough days. I really should exercise more than I do. I should meditate more than I do. Coffee and sugar are my friends. More friends I need to let go of. But, I'm taking my own advice and honoring the process. After all, whole life transformation doesn't happen overnight.

...Are you catching on to the theme here?

There are MANY ways to heal, balance and open your chakras. This book is going to focus on meditation with visualization, color and art therapy, crystal healing, aromatherapy with essential oils and FOOD. Food is my favorite. Did you know you can balance your chakras with different foods? Simply by eating them! Each chakra chapter includes a list of my favorite essential oils, spices, crystals and foods for chakra balancing. So, get ready, because a new you is just around the corner!

Alright, so here comes the part where I tell you about the alternative healing methods I have tried that worked for me.

Massage Therapy

It all kind of started here for me. That feeling of someone approaching my body with love and gentle energy. I grew up with people that weren't gentle with my body. I learned to hate touch, to fear being naked, to worship a life of distrust and a lack of intimacy. Allowing someone to touch my body- to let my guard down and trust in another human being to make me feel good- this was my first step. It took some practice. I spent the first few sessions refusing to take my underwear off and awkwardly filling the silence with lots of small talk. But now, oh how I love my massage sessions!

Essential Oils

I'm obsessed with essential oils and aromatherapy. I, myself, use doTerra essential oils because they are also safe to take internally. Please note that not every brand of essential oils is safe to take internally or even to use topically without dilution. I have sensitive skin and a sensitive digestive system and have no issues using this brand. My absolute favorite scents are peppermint and eucalyptus for a diffuser, lemon and ginger for internal use and lavender for my skin. If you decide to try this therapy, make sure you get a brand that is safe for internal and topical use. Do not buy them from a reseller, even if it's a "good" brand. I made the mistake once of ordering "doTerra" from Amazon- It. Was. Not. doTerra. Just go to the source. If its pricey, well, you get what you pay for. So, keep that in mind. And you only use a few drops each time, so 15ml might not seem like a lot but it lasts quite a while!

Urine Health Tonic

Simply stated, this is drinking your own urine. Yummy, delicious, warm pee. Like left-overs from your own body! Oh man, did you think I was serious? No, I don't do this you nutball! I just wanted to see if you are paying attention!! There are, however, people who subscribe to this idea. Sorry if I've offended you super fun urine-drinkers out there.

Reiki Energy Healing

You'll understand this more as you explore the chakras in this book. The basic concept here is that someone can approach your energy with theirs, filtrating the universe's energy. They remove negative energy from you and replace it with gentle, healing, loving energy from the universe. It's a hard concept to understand at first but I implore you to give it a shot with an open mind. Even if you don't understand it, it's a very relaxing experience.

Crystal Healing

Similar to Reiki, crystals carry an energy that can work with your own energy to heal you. There are crystals that correlate directly with each chakra and with specific intentions. In this book, I will include which crystals I work with for each chakra.

Meditation

You'll see meditations written for each chakra as you move forward in this book. Meditation helps you calm down, come to the present moment, and be mindful of the thought patterns you live in. Thought

So, what's the deal with Chakras, anyway!?

patterns can be positive or negative- and obviously, we don't want the negative ones sticking around. Negative thought patterns (such as negative self-talk- "I could never run a mile. I can't succeed. No one loves me")- they don't serve you in any way other than to hold you back.

Journaling

Get those thoughts out! Good ones and bad ones! Journaling helps you sift through those thoughts and feelings you are experiencing. Practice this often, and you'll see the difference it makes. This book, of course, includes journaling prompts to help you get started. You'll see what I'm talking about if you take those journaling prompts seriously.

Yoga

Ever seen an unhappy yogi? Yeah, me either. And if nothing else, you might be able to actually turn your head the way you're supposed to and touch your toes. Buti yoga, specifically, helped me find my confidence and turned off some of the negative feelings I associated with my sexuality (society has a way of stifling a woman's desires and feelings). We will get more into this when we explore the Sacral Chakra.

Leech Therapy

Not just for George Washington anymore! Leeches have made a comeback- I just place these little suckers on my skin and let them get fat on my blood. Just kidding! Are you paying attention?? (Although, again, some people do subscribe to this therapy- not for me though!)

Color Therapy & Art Therapy

In this book, we will explore color therapy in terms of balancing your chakras but scientifically, color therapy has been shown to resonate with certain receptors in your brain. Ever notice that every hospital tends to have light blue walls? This is no coincidence. Blue is associated with feeling calm and happy. Art expression has helped me work out some of my thoughts and feelings that I struggled with in terms of putting them into words. Art therapy was my go-to before discovering meditation and journaling. It is a way for me to release things I hold on to- good and bad- and put them in a physical, tangible outlet. Mandalas (like the ones you'll see in this book) were originally used for meditation but are also a form of art therapy.

Okay, so this about sums it up. Are you ready to dive in? To heal and balance using mandalas and color and crystals and energy and mindfulness? Don't worry, don't be afraid- there's no test at the end. And you can repeat these practices as many times as you want to! My suggestion is to take on just one chakra per week. Maybe read about it one night, try the journaling the next night and the mandala after that. Maybe do them all at once. Whatever feels natural to you. Don't stress yourself out about this; this will not be graded. The teacher will not test you on what you have learned. This is for YOU. For you to set aside time and energy for yourself. Time that you deserve. Love, after all, starts with you. Starts in your soul. So, practice some self-love today. You are worthy. You deserve this. You are safe. You are secure. You are loved.

Copyright ©KMRaposa.com all rights reserved 2019

Week 1
Root Chakra

Color: Red

Represents: Grounding, stability, support

Location: Base of your tailbone

Element: Earth

Essential Oils: Earthy smells like patchouli, sage, myrrh

Crystals: Anything dark or dark red- red tiger's eye, hematite, onyx, obsidian, tourmaline

Foods: Root vegetables (potatoes, carrots, beets, onions); Protein-rich foods like beans and peanut butter.

Spices: Paprika or pepper

Herbs: Dandelion Root, Ginger, Sage, Elderberry

So, what's the deal with Chakras, anyway!?

Copyright ©KMRaposa.com all rights reserved 2019

The root chakra is the energy center responsible for those feelings of being grounded, secure, safe, and allowing you to be in the present moment. This energy center or chakra is located at the base of your tailbone and is red in color. When this chakra is out of balance, you may feel airheaded or spacey. You may find it hard to concentrate and of course you may feel unfocused, unsafe, unworthy and/or unloved.

If you want to incorporate crystals or essential oils into this practice, you can pick up pretty much any dark colored stone- most of which are associated with grounding. My favorites are hematite, black tourmaline or red tiger's eye. Crystals are believed to hold energy and can transmit this healing energy to you when you are near them. Hey, it can't hurt, right? And, I figure, if plants hold energy, how is it any crazier to believe that minerals hold energy? So here I am collecting crystals and putting them in literally every corner of my house.

Aromatherapy- you know- the essential oil sniffing. This is all the rage on Facebook right now. You all know someone trying to sell you essential oils on your feed, right? Essential oils can help to soothe anxieties or provide an energy boost. I've included my favorite essential oils for healing and opening each chakra at the beginning of each chakra chapter. You can use these oils in body oil and topical use, some of them are great for your bath, and of course diffusing in a diffuser. For the root chakra, I use earthy smells- sandalwood, rosemary or maybe cedar. There are tons of crystals and oils you can use for this, but these are my favorites. For anxiety or to lift your spirits as opposed to grounding and calming you, I always go to peppermint. Peppermint is uplifting and motivating and helps you breathe easier by clearing your sinuses.

So, what's the deal with Chakras, anyway!?

Before moving on to the journaling and mandala portion of the Root Chakra, I want you to get yourself in the right space- physically, mentally and energetically. It's okay if your instinct is that you feel silly, or the thought crosses your mind that this is lame. That's normal. All I'm saying is to try it with an open mind. Come on, I know ya can. I know it seems a little silly to some of you, but what have you got to lose?

Take a moment to clear your mind. Find a quiet, safe space to sit in where you will not be interrupted. Shut your phone off. You don't need to Snapchat this experience. There's no location to check into on Facebook. Leave your phone in the other room if you're feeling brave. Photo evidence of this practice is not necessary. Of course, if you find peace in sharing this experience, this is your practice, so honor it. Do what you intuitively feel is right. No judgement here.

Your Root chakra is initially formed in your first year of life. You have no choice but to trust and rely on the people around you. You don't know better. Your root chakra continues to develop until about age 7, which is when our curiosity and propensity to adventure out of our comfort zones grows.

Before you begin journaling and filling in your mandala, lets journey into a quick meditation. When you are ready, close your eyes and imagine a red energy glowing and swirling at the base of your tailbone. When you can clearly see and/or feel that red energy, imagine roots, like tree roots, coming from the bottom of your feet down into the earth, grounding you and connecting you to earth's center.

Take at least 3-5 deep breathes, trying to focus only on the air coming in through your nose and out through your mouth.

Use the space provided below to write down any thoughts, feelings, or visualizations that you experienced during your meditation and breathing exercise. Try not to overthink it; just let the words flow out.

Copyright ©KMRaposa.com all rights reserved 2019

Affirmations

Say the following affirmations to yourself (out loud if you are feeling brave) you can manage to). Believe and know that they are true for you right now in this present moment:

I am safe.

I am protected.

I am grounded.

I am loved.

I am present.

Just keep repeating them to yourself over and over until you can feel that they are true. This may take only one time of repeating, or it could take 20. Or you could fall asleep tonight still not feeling it. Do not move on to the next chakra until you can recite these fully, knowing they are true for you.

When you are ready, move on to the journaling portion of this chakra. Answer the questions as honestly and fully as you can. I recommend working with the color red as much as possible- try to find a red pen or marker or crayon to journal with.

Journal Prompts

What is your earliest memory? Start with your earliest happy memory.

As a child, when did you the safest? Where were you? Who were you with? What were you doing?

How did your family (especially your parents) cope with stress when you were a child? What habits or belief patterns did you inherit from your family growing up?

So, what's the deal with Chakras, anyway!?

What made you feel unsafe as a child? What makes you feel unsafe now?

Do you often feel like you don't belong? In what situations do you feel like you don't belong?

Where do you feel like you DO belong?

Who makes you feel the safest, and/or the most loved?

What makes you feel safe now?

So, what's the deal with Chakras, anyway!?

What makes you feel the most loved, the happiest, and/or the most confident? Where is this place? Who is in this place? What are you doing in this place?

What are your top 5 favorite physical attributes?

If you are in a place where you do not cherish and appreciate your physical self, stay on this question until you can list at least 5 things.

How do you connect with your body?

How do you connect with your surroundings and with nature?

How do you connect with other people?

How can you share your gifts and strengths with others?

So, what's the deal with Chakras, anyway!?

Once you have completed your journaling, and you feel it is safe to do so, move on to the mandala on the next page. I have drawn each mandala in this book it be specific to each chakra. Because this is a beginner chakra exploration book, I will not delve into the symbols or element. I have hidden the chakra symbols, shapes and/or elements within each design. Color this mandala in with any medium you want but use only red tones. While coloring, try to keep yourself present; repeat those affirmations if you can. Reflect on what makes you feel safe and secure.

Do not move on to the next chakra until you completely feel you are ready to. Honor the process!

Write down any additional thoughts or feelings you are experiencing:

Download this print by visiting
www.KMRaposa.com

So, what's the deal with Chakras, anyway!?

Copyright ©KMRaposa.com all rights reserved 2019

Week 2
Sacral Chakra

Color: Orange

Represents: Passion, Joy, Confidence, Sexuality, Creativity

Location: Below belly button

Element: Water

Essential Oils: orange

Crystals: Rose Orange Calcite, Fire Agate, Snakeskin Agate

Food: Fruits like strawberries, melons, passion fruit, oranges, mangos.

Spices: Cinnamon

Herbs: Hibiscus tea, Calendula Flowers

Copyright ©KMRaposa.com all rights reserved 2019

Your Sacral Chakra is the energy enter responsible for your sexuality, creativity and emotions. Your sacral is located just below your belly button. Carnelian is my favorite crystal to work with for this chakra. I usually work with an orange essential oil too.

*Side note: the best part about using oils that are safe to take internally, is that you can put some orange right in your water or tea.

As a society, we have been brainwashed into being ashamed of our sexual desires, fantasies and needs. We have been told that sexuality should be expressed only in secret and that if we openly express our sexuality we are "easy, slutty, skanky, dirty." This goes for all genders and sexual orientations but, of course, some people feel this stigma more than others. Think back to when your childhood. How did you view your body? Sex? Following your dreams?

Answer the questions as honestly and fully as you can. I recommend working with orange as much as possible- try to find an orange pen or marker or crayon to journal with.

So, what's the deal with Chakras, anyway!?

Journal Prompts

What instances in your childhood helped shape your negative or positive view on sexuality, creativity, and your body?

Who do you feel most safe around? Who helps you grow and safely express yourself?

When do you feel the most passionate? What are you most passionate about?

Who are you most intimate with? This does not mean just sex- but who do you share your insecurities, passions, deepest thoughts and fears, and secrets with?

How do you express your sexuality? Do you express your sexuality in healthy ways?

What turns you on?

What turns you off?

How do you relax?

So, what's the deal with Chakras, anyway!?

Do you express your creativity often? How do you express your creativity?

How do you honor and love your own body?

What lessons are your relationships teaching you- not just romantic, but all relationships.

What do you want? What are your biggest dreams or most intimate desires?

Take a moment to clear your mind. Find a quiet, safe space to sit in where you will not be interrupted. Shut your phone off. No judgement here. Everyone meditates at different times and difference paces. If you can manage 15 or so minutes, I recommend listening to The Song of the Butterfly by Istvan Sky Kek Eg. It starts slow but has this amazing way of motivating and igniting passion as it picks up.

Bring to mind times when you feel most passionate. Bring to mind times where you feel the most confident in your sexuality and in expressing your sexual desires and needs. Bring to mind times when you feel most creative.

Where are you? What are you doing? Who are you with?

When you are able to answer these questions, close your eyes. Take at least 3-5 deep breathes; breathe in through your nose and out through your mouth. Picture a bright, hot orange energy orb circulating and filling the space just below your belly button. Allow it to move at its own pace. Stay here for a few minutes focusing on your breath and the image of this orange energy.

So, what's the deal with Chakras, anyway!?

Copyright ©KMRaposa.com all rights reserved 2019

Affirmations

Say the following affirmations to yourself, and believe that they are true for you right now in this present moment

I am a creative being.

My sexuality is vibrant.

It is safe to express my sexuality and creativity in healthy ways.

I am comfortable in my body.

My relationships are healthy and safe.

Sex is a sacred connection; I am safe enjoying sex.

I am passionate, radiant, beautiful and strong.

I am confident.

I am safe expressing myself creatively.

I am vibrant.

Just keep repeating them to yourself over and over until you can feel that they are true. This may take only one time of repeating, or it could take 20. Or you could fall asleep tonight still not feeling it.

Do not move on to the next chakra until you can recite these fully, knowing they are true for you.

Once you have completed your journaling and affirmations, and you feel it is safe to do so, move on to the mandala. Color this mandala in with any medium you want but use only orange tones. While coloring, try to keep yourself present; repeat those affirmations if you can. Reflect on what makes you feel safe and secure.

Do not move on to the next chakra until you completely feel you are ready to. Honor the process!

Use the space provided to write down any thoughts or feelings you are experiencing:

So, what's the deal with Chakras, anyway!?

Copyright ©KMRaposa.com all rights reserved 2019

Download this print by visiting

www.KMRaposa.com

So, what's the deal with Chakras, anyway!?

Copyright ©KMRaposa.com all rights reserved 2019

Week 3
Solar plexus chakra

Color: Yellow or gold

Represents: Wisdom & power

Location: Above belly button, below ribs

Element: Fire

Essential Oils: Lemon, Rosemary, Chamomile

Crystals: Citrine, Yellow Calcite, Pyrite

Food: Sunflower seeds, grains, flax seed, cheese

Spices: Ginger, turmeric, cumin

Herbs: Chamomile, Rosemary, Fennel Root

So, what's the deal with Chakras, anyway!?

Your solar plexus is located below your ribs but above and behind your belly button. It's yellow or gold in color. This is the energy center responsible for that feeling of confidence and self-esteem that we have. This is also the place of well-being and common sense.

Let's talk about your body for a second. I'm not going to go far into it in this first book, but each of our chakras are associated with different body parts and bodily functions. Your solar plexus is tied to your stomach and digestive function. Stomach issues are often associated with a solar plexus being out of balance. How is your stomach and digestion? Do you struggle with irregular bowel movement, feelings of bloating or cramping or too much gas? This can all be linked to a Solar Plexus that needs a little extra love!

Your solar plexus might be out of balance if you are over-confident, difficult, stubborn, unable to see the adverse side of situations. Your solar plexus might be out of balance if you also experience the polar opposite of this which is being unable to stand your grown when needed, often being taken advantage of, a lack of confidence or low self-esteem.

I'm not going to lie, I often struggle with this one. I also often struggle with stomach and digestive issues which is due to a combination of not always eating the right things and not taking care of my solar plexus. Hey, I told you in the first chapter that I'm not perfect, didn't I?

Journaling Prompts

So where do you feel more confident? Who are you around when you feel most confident?

Think back to when you were younger- how was your self-esteem? How did you see yourself? Were you confident?

What events or experiences shaped your feeling of self-worth or lack thereof?

How is your body image? Are you positive or negative about your body image?

Are there things about your body that you are unhappy with that you could easily change?

So, what's the deal with Chakras, anyway!?

How did your childhood affect your body image?

How does your adulthood affect your body image? How do you feel about your body? List positive and negative thoughts and feelings.

Does a confidence and body image affect your work life and personal relationships? List positive and negative observations.

Self-Esteem Boost Homework

Make a list of your own favorite PHYSICAL attributes (i.e. I am beautiful. I have beautiful green eyes. I love my small nose. I love my blonde hair. I love my freckles.)

Get a mirror

Look at yourself in the mirror; try to make eye contact. Attempt to do this for at least 5 minutes.

Say positive things to yourself while looking at yourself in the mirror.

DO NOT SAY NEGATIVE THINGS OUTLOUD

You may not be able to control your negative self-talk yet but try to focus on only positive observations.

Do this every day for 30 days.

Make a new list of positive physical attributes as often as you can or add to your original list.

Here's some space to begin your positive attributes list:

If you can, listen to the song Follow the Sun by Xavier Rudd- totally uplifting jam.

Find a quiet place, free from distraction. Bring to mind the color yellow. Place a yellow energy orb in your solar plexus which is just below your ribs above, and sort of behind your belly button. Allow your mind to see only yellow and gold and feel warmth in your belly. Stay here as long as you can/want. When you are ready, picture a yellow lotus flower sitting within your stomach. When you breathe in and out, this solar plexus flower opens and shuts. Every time your flower opens up, it grows brighter and bigger. Stay here for at least 5 deep breaths.

Use the space below to write down any thoughts, feelings, or visualizations that you experienced during your meditation and breathing exercise. Try not to overthink it; just let the words flow out.

Copyright ©KMRaposa.com all rights reserved 2019

Affirmations:

Say the following affirmations to yourself (come on, don't be a chicken- say them out loud). Know that they are true for you right here and now, in this present moment:

I am powerful

I am confident

I am comfortable in my own body

I release judgement of myself

I have high self-esteem

I am motivated

I use my power for good

I am worthy

I am open to new ways of doing things

I am in control of how I respond to situations

I have inner peace

I come from a place of authentic power

I set boundaries with ease

I practice self-care and self-respect

I express myself, my passions and my desires confidently

Once you have completed your journaling and affirmations, and you feel it is safe to do so, move on to the mandala. Color this mandala in with any medium you want but use only yellow tones. While coloring, try to keep yourself present; repeat those affirmations if you can. Reflect on what makes you feel safe and secure.

Do not move on to the next chakra until you completely feel you are ready to. Honor the process!

Download this print by visiting

www.KMRaposa.com

Copyright ©KMRaposa.com all rights reserved 2019

Week 4
Heart Chakra

Color: Green

Represents: Love, Forgiveness, Compassion

Location: Heart/Chest

Element: Air

Essential Oils: Rose; Lime; Jasmine

Crystals: Rose Quartz; Emerald

Food: Leafy greens like spinach

Spices: Thyme, Cilantro, Basil

Herbs: Hawthorn Berry tea

Copyright ©KMRaposa.com all rights reserved 2019

The Sanskrit word for the heart chakra is "anahata." Anahata translates into "unhurt, unstuck or unbeaten." Pretty intense wording right here, isn't it? But think about what holds you back when it comes to love or accepting love. Are you stuck? Are you or have you been hurt in the past?

Do you know if your heart chakra is stuck? Do you feel lonely or shy? Do you feel like it is hard to empathize with others? It's not necessarily bad to lead with your head over your heart, if heart is present; however, when you lead without your heart, decisions lack consideration for others, compassion and love. Maybe your heart chakra is overpowering your energy. Do you feel jealous or judgmental of others? Have you fallen into a life of severe codependency? RED FLAG!

Your heart chakra can be unbalanced because of so many things in love- jealousy, a broken relationship with another person, having toxic people in your life, death of a loved one. No one is immune, which is why it's so important to be able to heal your heart chakra on your own.

Before you are ready to achieve balance within relationships with others, you have to find balance within your own heart space. You must able to accept yourself and offer yourself unconditional acceptance and love.

Let's balance that out!

Find a quiet place where you feel safe and secure- somewhere you won't be interrupted for the duration of your practice. Take a few moments to focus on your breath and the natural way it flows. At this point, do not try to alter your current breathing pattern. Just acknowledge your natural air flow. When you are ready and able to quiet your mind, slow down your breath. Take deeper inhalations and when you breathe out, try to breathe out as fully as you can- pull your stomach as far to your spine as you can.

Allow your body to relax. Focus on each part individually. Start with your feet, allow your feet and toes to hang naturally and comfortably. This practice can be done sitting down, standing up, laying down... any way you feel comfortable and safe. Move up your legs and allow your shins, knees and thighs to loosen and relax.

Move up to your pelvis, stomach and chest. Still focusing on taking those slow, deep breaths, allow these areas to relax and loosen. If your feel gassy, let it go!! This is not a time to hold in anything. I'm serious- you might think I'm kidding- but fart if you need to! This is a sign from your body that you are ready to release. Take some deep breaths as you relax your chest, your arms, hands and fingers. Many of us hold tension in our shoulders and neck, make sure to release this, stretch your neck, move your head side to side and relax. Finally, relax all the muscles in your face. Unclench your jaw and release your tongue from the top of your mouth if you are holding it there. Move your eyebrows up and down to release any tension you are holding in your forehead.

When you are ready- close your eyes and imagine a green, warm energy orb circulating in your chest. Filling you with warmth. Stay here as long as you feel comfortable, until you feel balanced and open and ready to take on the journaling part of this chakra balancing experience.

Journal it out!

This is so important for the heart chakra. Journaling and expressing your feelings, conveying them anyway you feel comfortable and safe- is SO important. You MUST release your feelings-good and bad. I often use art as my expression tool, but journaling is a huge component as well. JOURNAL FREQUENTLY. You may not feel comfortable journaling daily or even weekly, but if you can find time to journal once a month at least, I highly recommend it. Try to aim for a full moon or new moon if you can. I also recommend working with the color green when aiming to heal or open your heart chakra.

Use this space provided to write down any thoughts or feelings you are experiencing:

So, what's the deal with Chakras, anyway!?

Journal Prompts

Reflect on your experience during your heart chakra meditation. What colors did you see? What did you feel- positive and negative?

Did you learn anything about yourself during this exercise?

How was love expressed to you and around you as a child? Think about your family growing up. What made you feel loved as child; who made you feel loved and how did people show love to you and around you growing up?

List qualities you have that other people may not like- i.e. being overly critical, being chronically late to events, being self-absorbed.
Continue writing until you cannot think of anything else. When you are finished writing, read the list to yourself while looking yourself in the mirror but add "I love and accept myself just the way I am" after each statement.

Write a list of positive things, attributes you admire, about yourself. I recommend writing this in sort of a letter form- as if you are writing a letter to a friend- about how much you love and appreciate yourself. This sounds easy, but we all know it's not always easy to speak to yourself kindly. This is not bragging. This is not self-centered. You are showing yourself love that you truly deserve and are worthy of. Continue writing until you cannot think of anything else.

How do you show yourself love?

How do you show others love?

Are you compassionate toward others?

Are others compassionate toward you?

Do you listen to others without judgement?

Do you feel you can give and accept love freely?

What holds you back from giving and accepting love freely?

List something(s) you can do TODAY to start healing your heart chakra- to be able to give and accept love freely.

Affirmations

Say the following affirmations to yourself knowing they are true for you today, in this present moment:

I give love freely

I am full open to receiving love

I am worthy of love

I forgive myself

I forgive others

I release judgement of myself

I release judgements of others

I am grateful for all of my blessings

I create loving and supporting relationships

I am safe loving others

My heart is healed and free from past traumas

I give and receive love effortlessly and unconditionally

Once you have completed your journaling and affirmations, and you feel it is safe to do so, move on to the mandala. Color this mandala in with any medium you want but try to only use green and/or pink tones. While coloring, try to keep yourself present; repeat those affirmations if you can. Reflect on what makes you feel safe and secure.

Do not move on to the next chakra until you completely feel you are ready to. Honor the process!

Use the space provided to write down any additional thoughts or feelings you had during this experience:

Download this print by visiting

www.KMRaposa.com

Copyright ©KMRaposa.com all rights reserved 2019

Week 5
Throat Chakra

Color: Blue

Location: Throat, mouth, ears

Element: Ether/Space

Essential Oils: Eucalyptus or Peppermint

Crystals: Sodalite; Lapis Lazuli; Angelite; Celestite

Food: Water! Hydrate my friend! Herbal Teas

Herbs: Lemon Balm or Eucalyptus tea

Copyright ©KMRaposa.com all rights reserved 2019

Journal Prompts

Oh, here it comes- my favorite chakra! My throat chakra and I have become awfully close this past year. A chakra I used to ignore, just like I ignored my need to communicate my needs, thoughts, feelings, desires... We are going to jump right into journaling on this one. Let's start communicating!

As you work through this questions and exercises, don't be afraid to be completely honest with yourself. No one will read this. No one will judge this. This is yours. Rereading what you write will help you build awareness of your strengths and weaknesses. By being aware, you take ownership of your feelings and thoughts and this will help you identify where you need to grow.

Your throat chakra begins to really develop between ages 7-12. Consider, for a moment, how communication was for you during this time. Were you encouraged to communicate? To make noise through instruments or express yourself through art or dance? Who or what, if anything, held you back? Who or what assisted you in expressing yourself?

How is your relationship with communication? Are you often told to speak up? Or shut up? We live in a strange society where if you speak up you're often told to shut up (especially as a woman)- you're told you are too demanding or too needy or too loud. And if you don't speak up, you become a pawn in everyone else's life and you are just pushed around and taken advantage of- or worse- ignored. Where do you stand?

Do you speak your truth?

Do you express what you believe to be true? Or do you stay silent and avoid speaking your truth? Why? What holds you back from speaking your truth? Is it judgement from others, or fear, or not wanting to be a "burden?"

Do you express yourself? Freely? Art, music, speaking, dancing- how do you express yourself? If you don't, we need to plan to start expressing!!

Imagine for a moment, that you freely express yourself. You have no fear or hesitation in this moment. What would you say? Who would you say it to? How would you express yourself right now if you had any outlet available to you

Your throat chakra is not just located in your throat. It is located in your mouth, in your ears… True and honest communication is not just speaking your truth, but also listening actively to others. Listening without judgement. Listening with compassion.

Do you listen to others actively? Do you listen with compassion and without judgement?

Before you journal the prompt below, I'd like you to take some time to clear your mind and meditate. Imagine a blue energy orb swirling in your throat, filling your mouth and overflowing out your ears. Imagine that this cool, blue energy grows brighter and even travels through your body with each breath you take. Take at least 5 deep inhales and exhales as you envision this blue energy traveling with your oxygen through your entire body.

If you could communicate anything to any person or people, what would you communicate and to whom? Why haven't you communicated this? What is holding you back? Make an action plan today to express these thoughts and feelings to that person or people.

Copyright ©KMRaposa.com all rights reserved 2019

Affirmations

Focus on the following affirmations and say them to yourself knowing that they are true for you right now in this present moment.

I communicate my feelings, needs, desires and thoughts with confidence

I am able to clearly express my needs

I speak my truth

My voice is heard

I am comfortable in silence

I set clear boundaries

I listen with compassion

I speak words which reflect my loving heart

I am balanced in expressing my thoughts, emotions and needs

I forgive myself for things I have said or not said and release doubt

My voice is important

I honor my true voice and speak only with love

My thoughts and words are positive and true

Once you have completed your journaling and affirmations, and you feel it is safe to do so, move on to the mandala. Color this mandala in with any medium you want but use only blue tones. While coloring, try to keep yourself present; repeat those affirmations if you can. Reflect on what makes you feel safe and secure.

Do not move on to the next chakra until you completely feel you are ready to. Honor the process!

Use the space below to write down any thoughts, feelings, or visualizations that you experienced during your meditation and breathing exercise. Try not to overthink it; just let the words flow out.

Download this print by visiting

www.KMRaposa.com

Week 6
Third Eye Chakra

Color: Indigo/Purple

Represents: Intuition, Knowledge, Trust

Location: Top of your nose, between your eyebrows

Element: All Elements Combined/Light

Essential Oils: Lavender

Crystals: Purple Fluorite; Amethyst; Lepidolite

Food: blackberries, raspberries, blueberries, grapes

Spices/Herbs: Mint and Lemon

Your third eye helps guide your intuition. It helps you to know, naturally, what the right thing to do is. It helps you to know you are part of something bigger, and that your journey is supported. It allows you to trust yourself and your natural instincts. You know that "inner voice" you have? Time to learn to trust it!

Before tackling your journal questions, take a moment to clear your mind. Take at least 5 deep inhales & exhales. When you are ready, imagine a dark purple energy orb circulating or pulsing right at the top of your nose, between your eye brows. This is where your third eye is located. Stay here for a few minutes focusing on your breath and connecting with this purple energy.

Affirmations

Say the following affirmations as though they are true for you, right now, in this present moment:

I trust my intuition

I am wise and connected with my subconscious

I listen to my inner wisdom

I understand and learn from my previous, current and future experiences

I forgive myself for past mistakes

I love and accept myself

I am open to learning from others

I am open to inspiration

I am at peace

I am love

So, what's the deal with Chakras, anyway!?

Journal Prompts:

(Try to write with a purple pen, marker, pencil, crayon if possible.)
Do you trust yourself? Why or why not?

How does a lack of self-trust affect your life, your decisions, your relationships?

Do you believe that you have an inner voice or guidance that shows you the right steps to take?

How would completely trusting yourself and your intuition make your life better? How would it affect your relationships with others?

What is your experience with intuition? When you were younger, were you encouraged to trust your intuitive feelings?

Do you have vivid dreams? Is it easy or difficult for your to recall your dreams in detail?

Once you have completed your journaling and affirmations, and you feel it is safe to do so, move on to the mandala. Color this mandala in with any medium you want but use only purple tones. While coloring, try to keep yourself present; repeat those affirmations if you can. Reflect on what makes you feel safe and secure.

Do not move on to the next chakra until you completely feel you are ready to. Honor the process!

Copyright ©KMRaposa.com all rights reserved 2019

Download this print by visiting

www.KMRaposa.com

Copyright ©KMRaposa.com all rights reserved 2019

Week 7
Crown Chakra

Color: White

Represents: Oneness, Wholeness, Balance with the Universe

Location: Top of your head

Element: Thought

Essential Oils: Frankincense, Jasmine, Cedarwood

Crystals: Crystal quartz, selenite, Iceland spar

Food: (Traditionally, fasting and detoxing are beneficial for your crown chakra); Lavender tea

Spices/Herbs: Lavender, lotus root

Copyright ©KMRaposa.com all rights reserved 2019

Your crown chakra influences your ability to hold a deeper understanding of yourself beyond the physical or material world. It connects us with the universe and helps us to see the bigger picture. Our thoughts, feelings, actions, and words all affect everything around us and even the smallest thing has a ripple effect.

Before you begin with affirmations and journaling, lets get in the right mindset! Take at least 5 deep inhales and exhales. Stay here until you can clear your mind and focus on the following visualization.

When you are ready, close your eyes and picture a white lotus flower sitting on top of your head. When you breathe in and breathe out, this lotus flower opens and shuts. And when this lotus flower opens, little white sparks gently float out of it and trickle down your body. These sparks ignite each of the chakras you have journeyed through in the former chapters of this book, turning each chakra from their regular color to white. Stay here, visualizing this lotus flower and its magical sparks until you feel ready to move on to your affirmations and journaling.

You have worked with your intuition and listening to your body and mind in the last chapter (3rd eye) so trust the feeling when you think you are ready to move on. It is ok to stay in this moment with your crown chakra lotus flower as long as you want!

Copyright ©KMRaposa.com all rights reserved 2019

Affirmations

Say the following affirmations to yourself knowing they are true for you, right now, in this present moment:

I trust myself

I trust in the universe

I am worthy of love from the universe

I am complete

I matter

I am part of a bigger community

I am perfect just the way I was created

I receive guidance from my higher self

I have purpose; I know my purpose

I am light

I am part of the universal flow

I am love

So, what's the deal with Chakras, anyway!?

Journaling Prompts:

Is your spiritual life balanced? What does having a spiritual life mean to you?

Do you consider yourself to be wise and insightful?

Do you feel a strong connection with others and a Higher Power?

So, what's the deal with Chakras, anyway!?

Do you know that your life has purpose, and do you know what that purpose is?

Did you easily answer "yes" to the above questions? If you did- you can skip this chapter because that means you are showing strong signs that your crown chakra is balanced! I, however, will be continuing because a few of those left me stumped.

Do you struggle with your spirituality (at least at times)? Do you feel unbalanced in your spirituality?

Do you ever fear mortality or death?

How does this fear get in the way of you living your true and honest life?

Do you ever feel alone in the universe?

Do you ever struggle with feelings of being unloved by or angry at a higher power?

Okay, now we're talking. The crown chakra is a tough one, guys! I don't have all the answers- sorry! I'm still working on this chakra too.

Once you have completed your journaling and affirmations, and you feel it is safe to do so, move on to coloring your lotus. Color this in with any medium you want and any colors you want. While coloring, try to keep yourself present; repeat those affirmations if you can. Reflect on what makes you feel safe and secure.

Gratitude List:

Use this page to list all the things you are grateful for!

So, what's the deal with Chakras, anyway!?

Copyright ©KMRaposa.com all rights reserved 2019

Download this print by visiting
www.KMRaposa.com

So, what's the deal with Chakras, anyway!?

Copyright ©KMRaposa.com all rights reserved 2019

Local Resources

Here are some of my favorite local spots that support energy healing, crystal healing, essential oils and dried herbs, teas, and tonics:

Solshine Yoga Studio New Bedford, MA
SolshineYoga.org
Sacred Lotus Westport, MA
Facebook.com/SacredLotusofWestport
Euphoria Day Spa Fairhaven, MA
EuphoriaDay-Spa.com
Divine Massage Mattapoisett and New Bedford, MA
DivineMassageMa.com
Bilo Herbs Westport, MA
BiloHerbs.com
Strawberry Moon Dartmouth, MA
Etsy.com/shop/strawberrymoon3
Mattapoisett Wellness Center
MattapoisettWellness.com
People's Pressed New Bedford, MA
PeoplesPressed.com
Divinely Balanced Holistic Healing New Bedford, Ma
DivinelyBalancedHolisticHealing.com

Made in the USA
Middletown, DE
22 August 2019